Drawing & Coloring
for Calm

Wendy Piersall

Published by Yellow Pear Press, a division of Mango Publishing Group, Inc.

Interior Illustration: Wendy Piersall
Cover Design/Book Layout by: Lilia Garvin

For permission requests, please contact the publisher at:
Mango Publishing Group
2850 S Douglas Road, 4th Floor
Coral Gables, FL 33134 USA
info@mango.bz

For special orders, quantity sales, course adoptions and corporate sales, please email the publisher at sales@mango.bz. For trade and wholesale sales, please contact Ingram Publisher Services at customer.service@ingramcontent.com or +1.800.509.4887.

Drawing and Coloring For Calm

ISBN: (p) 978-1-64250-901-4
BISAC: ART010000, ART / Techniques / Drawing

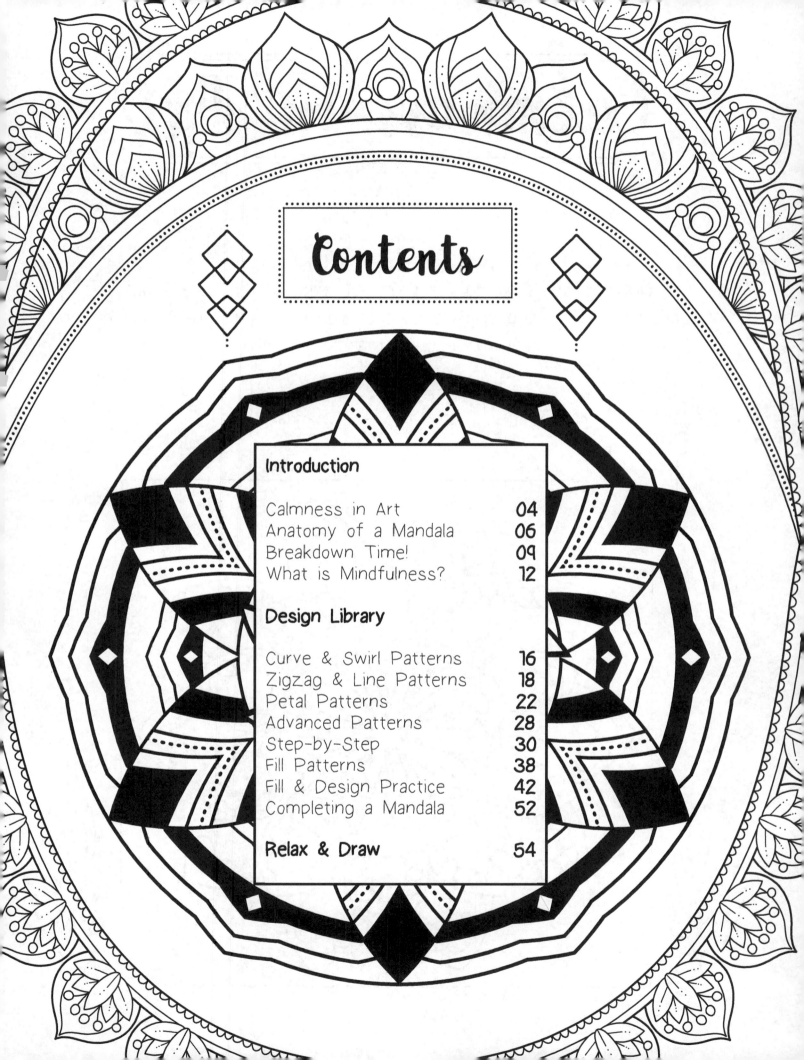

Contents

Calmness in Art

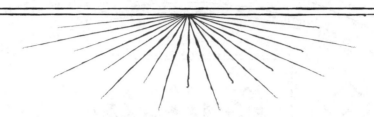

In *Drawing and Coloring for Calm*, we take all the stress out of doodling, drawing, and coloring so that you can simply relax and enjoy making beautiful mandala artwork.

But first: what is a mandala?

A **Mandala**, which comes from the Sanskrit word for "circle," is a spiritual symbol that represents the universe in Buddhism and Hinduism. Interestingly, these beautiful, radial designs have also been found in Christianity, as well as Mesoamerican cultures. Both Mayan and Aztec civilizations depicted calendars with mandalas.

Often, mandalas are used as meditation aids. If you find yourself relaxing while drawing mandalas, don't be surprised!

Together, we are going to learn how to design mandalas using radial grids. You can make your designs with pencils, pens, colored pencils, or other materials—don't feel limited!

It's time to look at our first mandala grid.

Are you ready?

Let's get started!

Anatomy of a Mandala
This is a mandala grid!

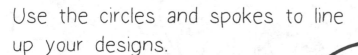

You'll be using a grid to guide your mandala drawings throughout this book. The grid will help you to make even and proportional designs in every mandala you draw!

I always find it easiest to start in the middle of the circle and draw designs working from the center outward. Start by drawing shapes or lines on your mandala grid, as shown below.

Use the circles and spokes to line up your designs.

Notice there are 3 "layers" to this mandala to the left that line up with the three circles on the grid.

The first inside layer is 6 teardrops in the center.

The second layer is 6 rounded triangles in the middle.

The third layer is 6 rounded diamond shapes on the outside.

Easy enough so far, right?

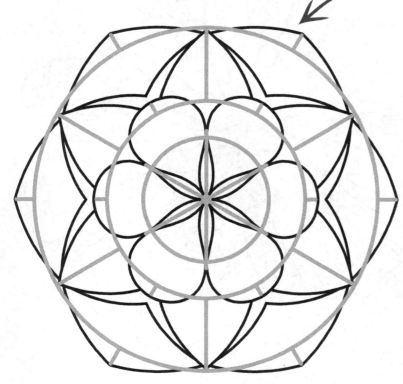

After you've drawn out the large shapes on the layers of your mandala, you can add as many details as you want. For this mandala, I started by adding some dark accents to each layer.

This is a fun place to start adding colors if you want, too!

Next, I've started adding some more lines within the shapes. Notice that each section of each layer is the same all the way around the mandala.

If you get stumped on what details to add, I have plenty of pages of patterns, fills, and other designs you can use later in this book. Right now, I just want you to see how to build details into your drawing as you progress.

There is *no right or wrong way* to draw a mandala! Add as much color or detail as you want. I added a few more lines, dots, and dark accents to my mandala. Notice that a drawing that started out very simple now looks very detailed and intricate with every new addition.

Remember that every <u>easy</u> step along the way was simply adding a few lines, dots, or filled-in shapes!

See the finished mandala below!

Breakdown Time!

We've learned what a mandala is, and how to use grids to help us create beautiful pieces of art. Using that knowledge, we can look at mandalas and understand how to piece them together.

Starting from the center, we see petal designs, lines, triangles, and zigzag patterns with dot accents. There are four examples of mandala breakdowns on the next few pages.

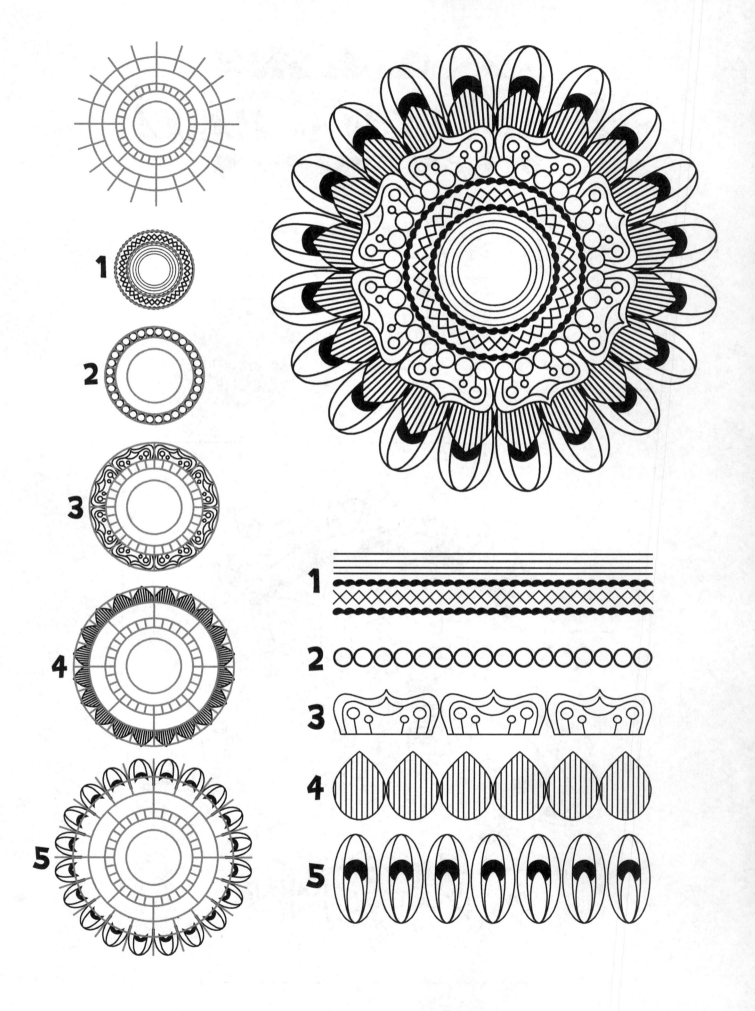

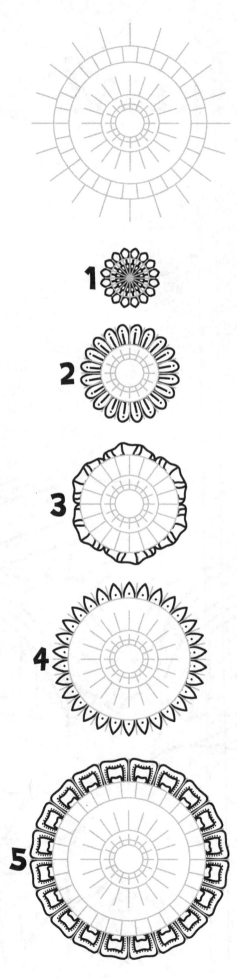

1

2

3

4

5

What is Mindfulness?

Mindfulness is "the state of being conscious or aware of something."

In everyday language, mindfulness means focusing our attention on the present moment, and letting our thoughts and feelings float by without getting attached to them.

Put even more simply, mindfulness is the art of noticing what's happening in the present moment.

When you stay in the present moment, you can reduce stress and anxiety surrounding both past and future events.

Drawing and coloring help ground you in the present, keeping you focused simply on creating something beautiful.

Being Present

As you use this book, you may notice that thoughts go in and out of your mind while you are drawing. As you continue to doodle and draw, your attention will continue to be focused on your work, rather than getting caught up in your thoughts.

Sometimes, you may want to write down the thoughts that go through your mind while drawing. We've provided coloring pages throughout the book for you to take a break to notice what you're thinking about. Once you're done coloring, you can go back to drawing.

When you do this, you are being present in the moment rather than thinking about the past or future. You will probably feel relaxed and centered when you practice mindfulness. And the more you practice, the more you can feel relaxed and centered in your everyday life.

Design Library

Curve & Swirl Patterns

Going forward, we're going to explore different patterns that you can use when creating your own mandalas.

Let's look at some curves & swirls.

For some extra fun, you can color in our example mandalas!

When designing your first mandalas, you can refer back to patterns from any of these example sections, mixing and matching to create something beautiful.

Curve & Swirl Patterns

Zigzag & Line Patterns

You can vary the thickness of your lines, zigzag them around, and use creative patterns to create stunning mandalas that look way more complicated than they actually are!

Zigzag & Line Patterns

Zigzag & Line Patterns

Petals

Petal Patterns

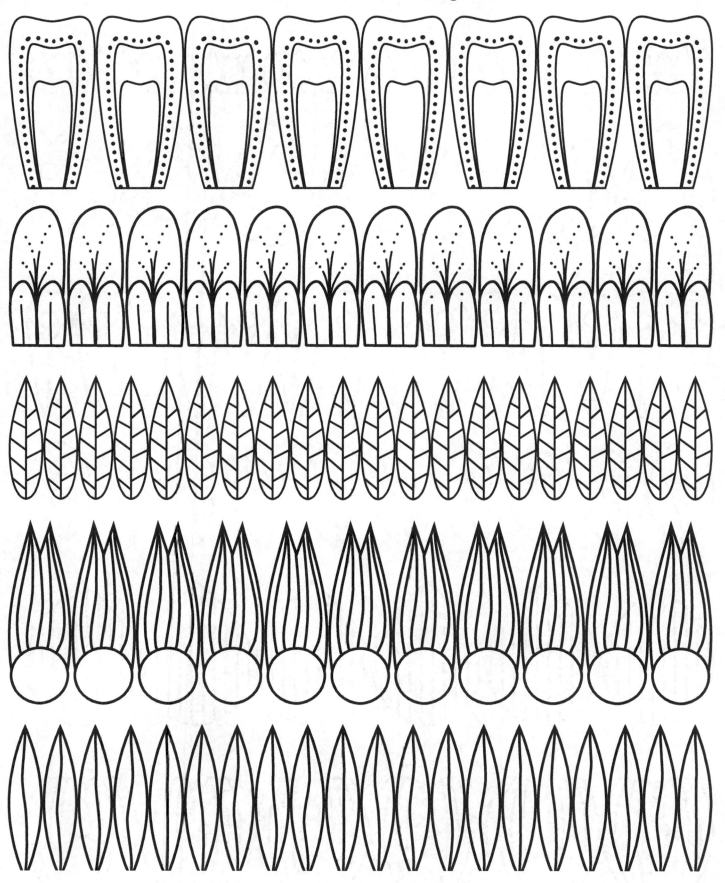

Petal Patterns

Petal Patterns

Advanced Patterns

Step-by-Step

Some patterns are more complicated than others. If you decide you want to include intricate designs, don't worry! It isn't difficult at all. Once you draw the skeleton of your mandala, you'll likely be left with open areas. You can fill these sections with repeating fill patterns, like the ones shown over the next few pages. Follow the step-by-step examples to include these beautiful patterns in your own mandalas.

Afterward, you can practice applying fill patterns to several of our example mandalas, like these two. Use black & white, or color!

When drawing for calm, don't worry.

Just go one line at a time!

Fill Patterns

Fill Patterns

Fill & Design Practice

Over the next several pages, you will find mandala designs with empty shapes and sections. This is your opportunity to practice filling in a mandala once you've created its major shapes. You can use fill patterns from the Design Library, or create your own!

43

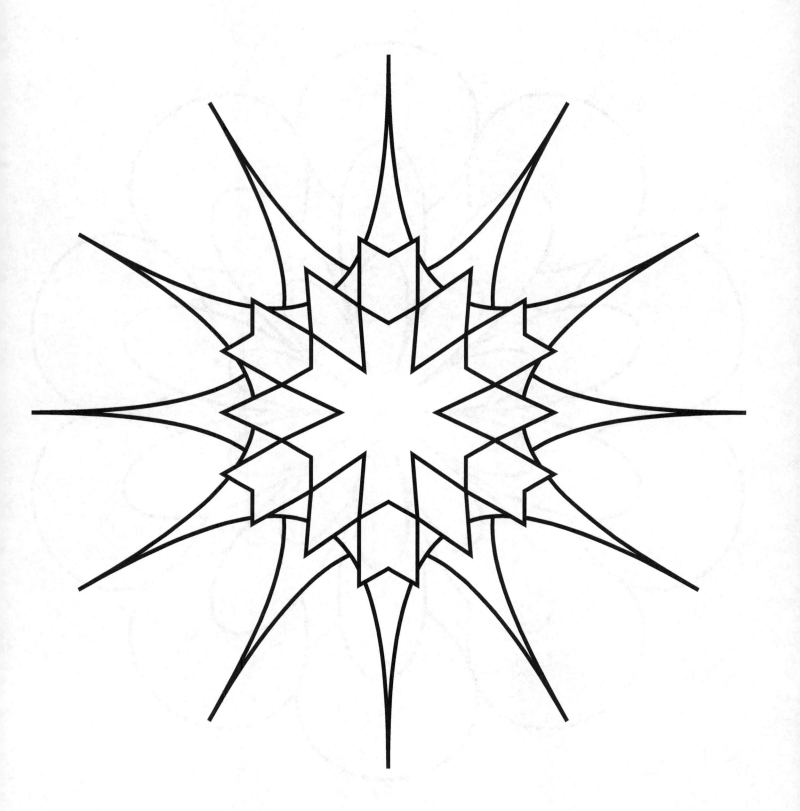

Completing a Mandala

It's almost time to make your own mandalas.

You can use a grid to create designs, like the one below, by repeating patterns. These designs can be zigzags, swirls, petals, or other imaginative advanced patterns. If after designing your mandala you are left with unfilled areas, you can complete them with fill patterns.

Take a crack at finishing the mandala below!

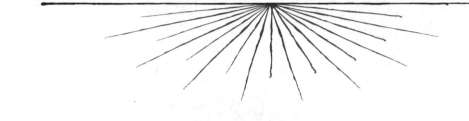

Relax & Draw

We've explored how to use mandala grids, looked at examples of mandalas, and gone over various design elements including curved patterns, zigzags, petals, advanced, step-by-step, and fill patterns. You can use these skills going forward, and can always flip back to find ideas!

You've got this. It's time to make your own mandalas.

Have Fun!

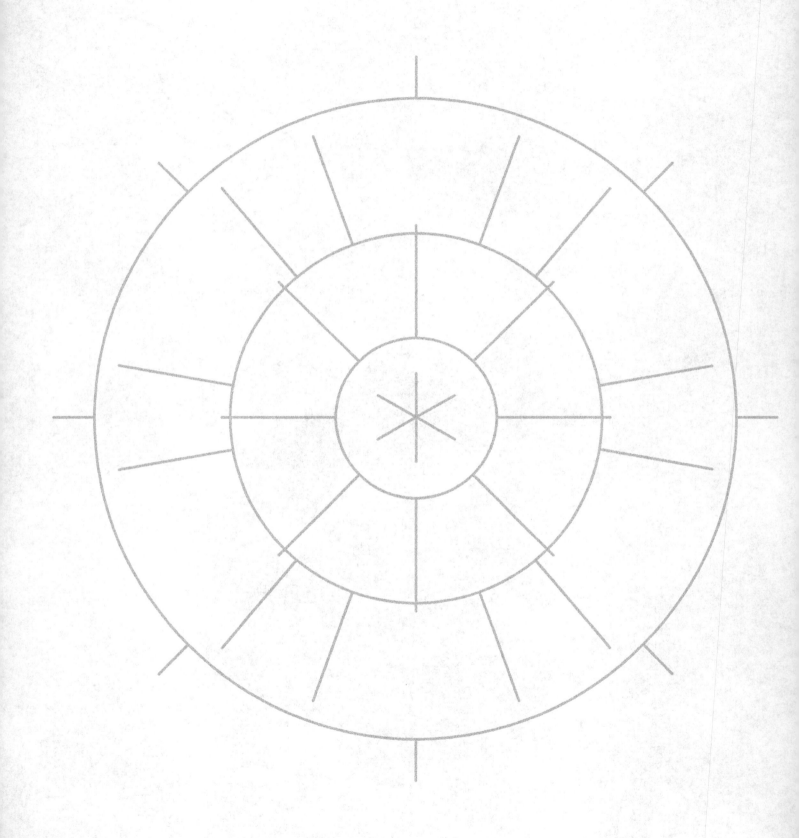

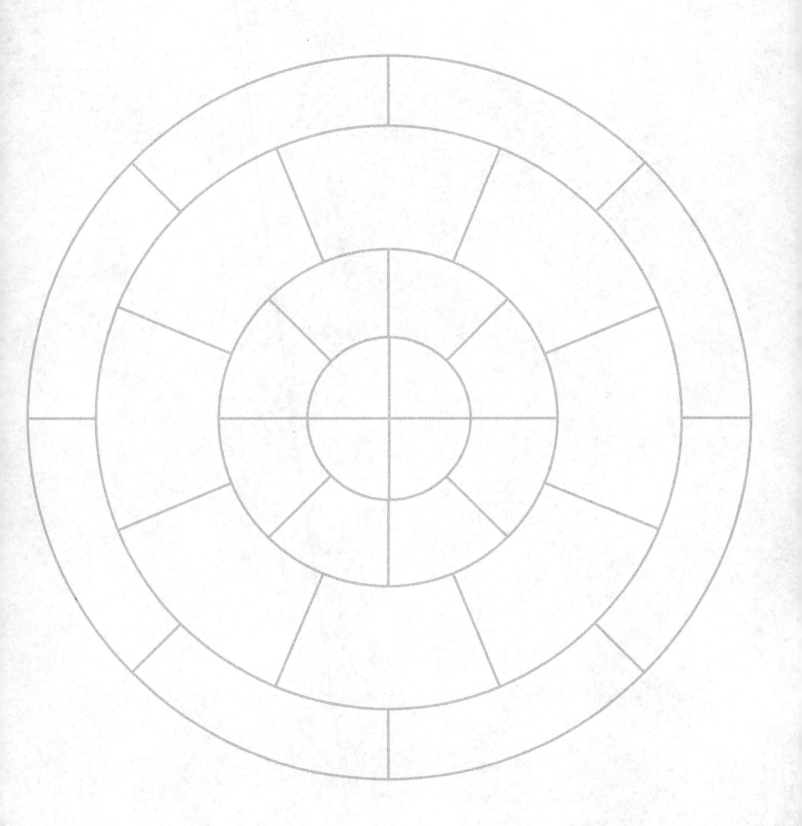

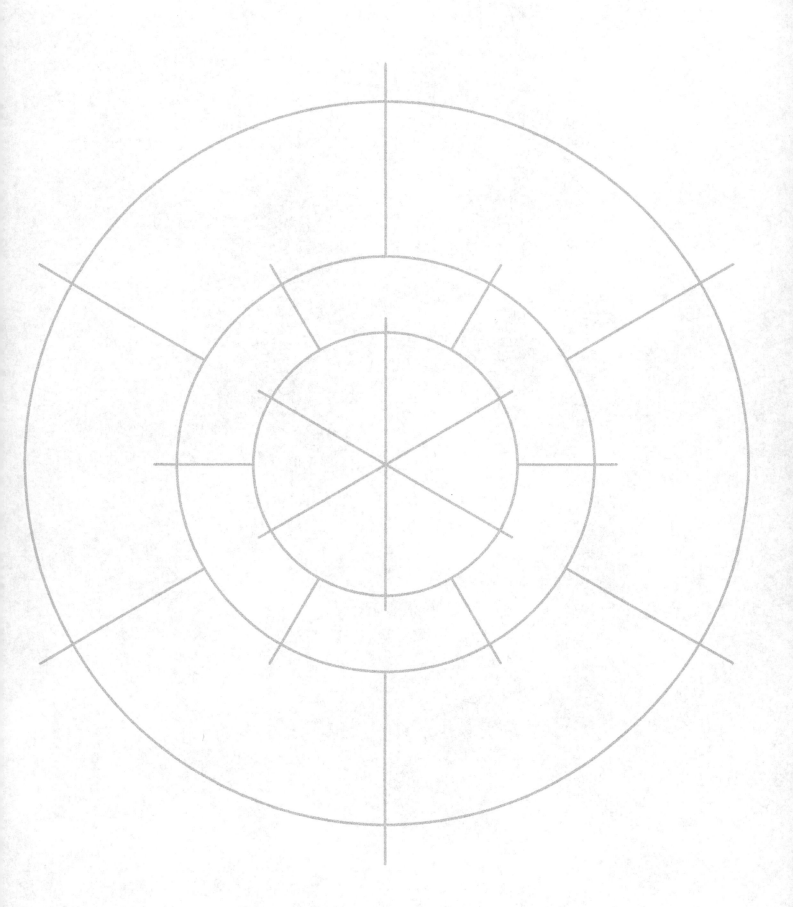

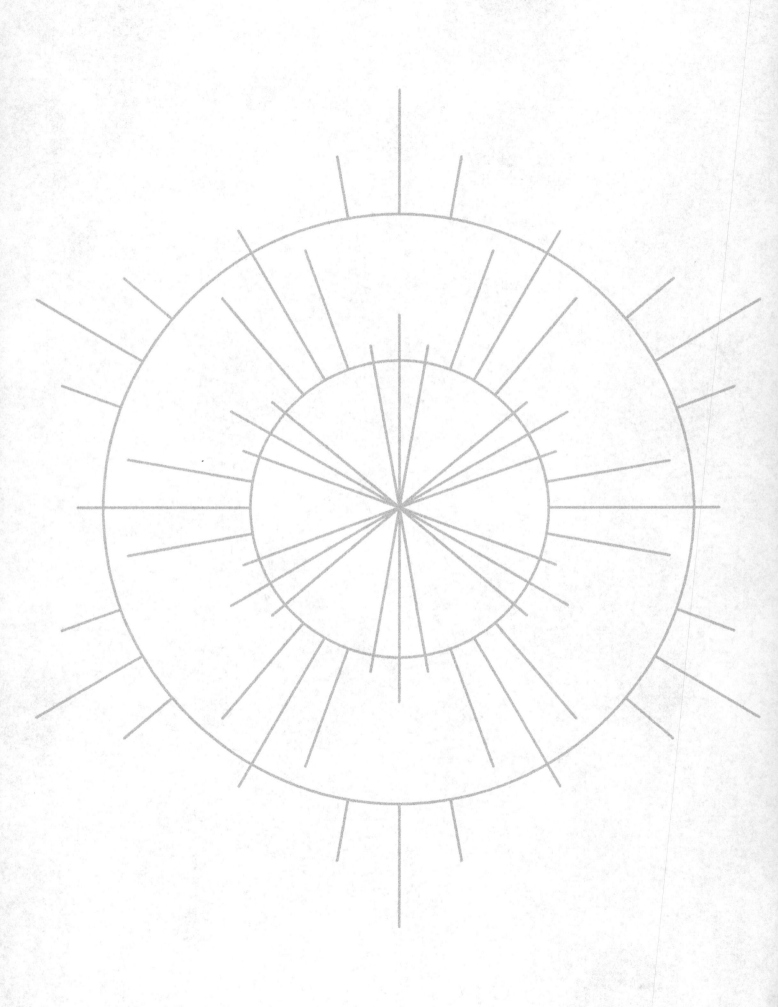

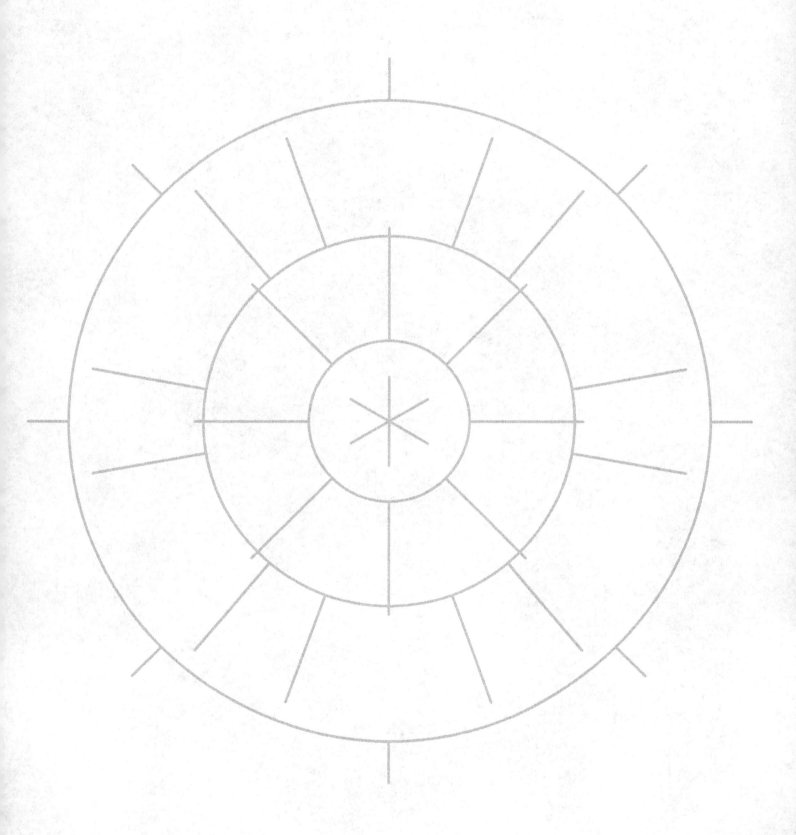

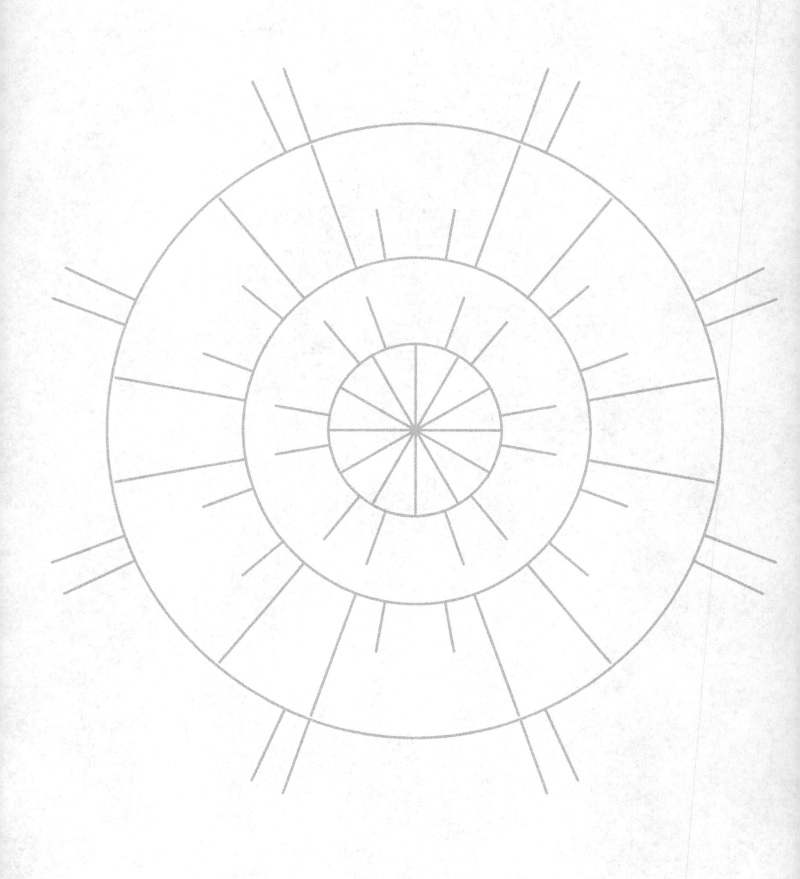

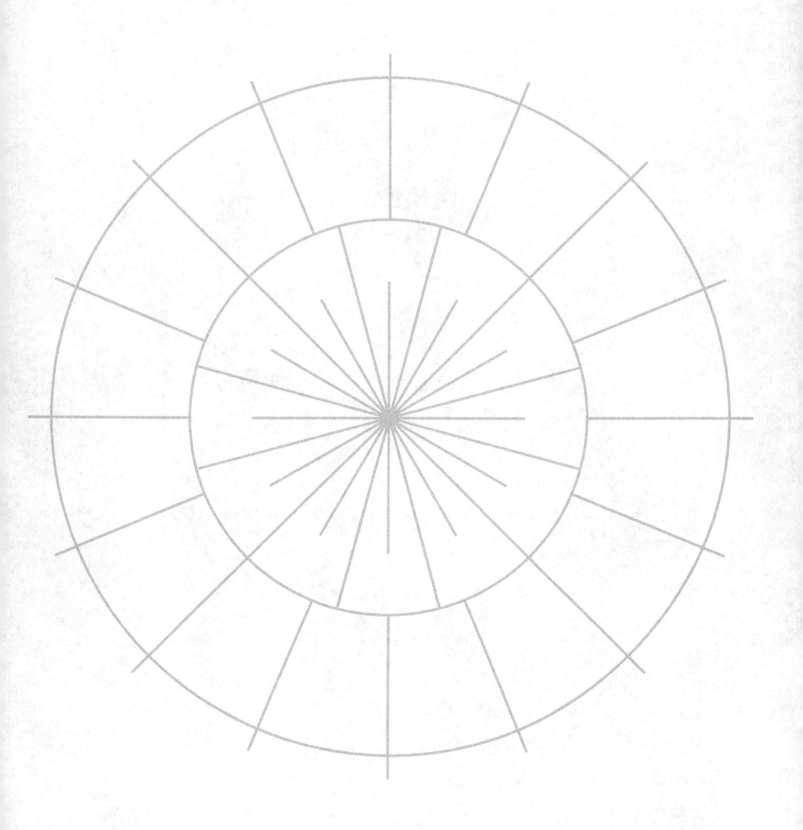

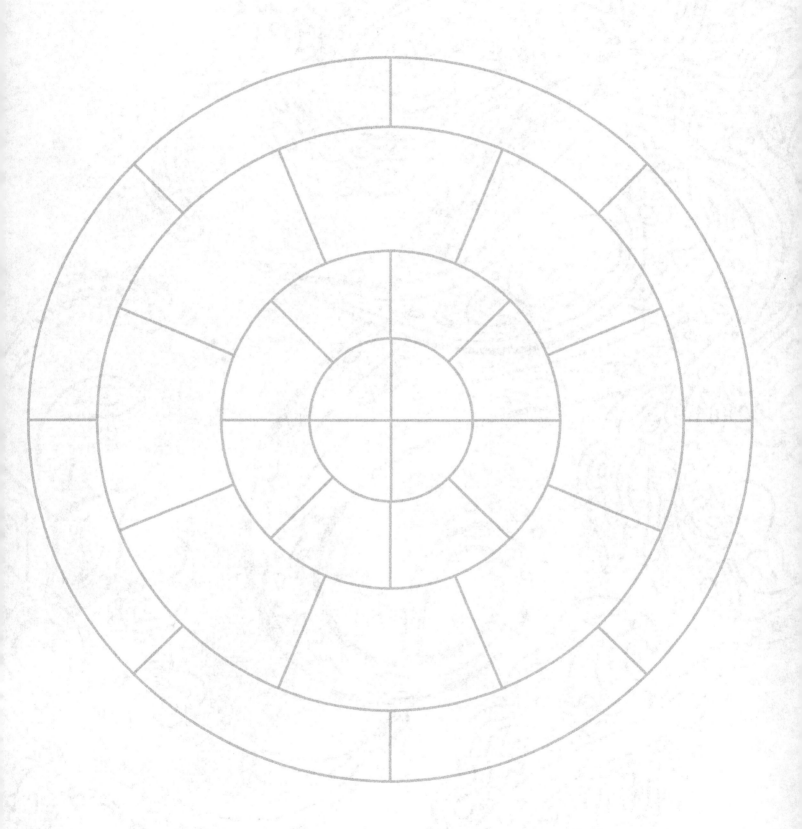

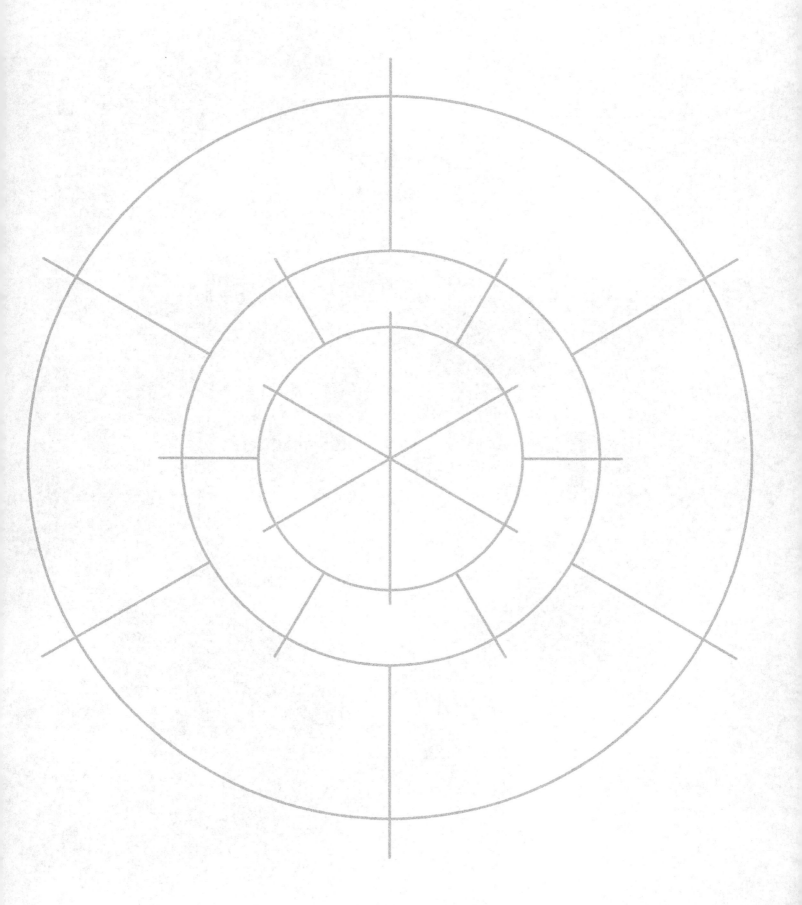

yellow pear press

Yellow Pear Press, established in 2015, publishes inspiring, charming, clever, distinctive, playful, imaginative, beautifully-designed lifestyle books, cookbooks, literary fiction, notecards, and journals with a certain joie de vivre in both content and style. Yellow Pear Press books have been honored by the Independent Publisher Book (IPPY) Awards, National Indie Excellence Awards, Independent Press Awards, and International Book Awards. Reviews of our titles have appeared in Kirkus Reviews, Foreword Reviews, Booklist, Midwest Book Review, San Francisco Chronicle, and New York Journal of Books, among others. Yellow Pear Press joined forces with Mango Publishing in 2020, both with the vision to continue publishing clever and innovative books. The fact that they're both named after fruit is a total coincidence.

We love hearing from our readers, so please stay in touch with us and follow us at:
Facebook: Yellow Pear Press
Twitter: @yellowpearpress
Instagram: @yellowpearpress
Pinterest: yellowpearpress
Website: www.yellowpearpress.com

Wendy Piersall has been creating content for aspiring artists and professional creatives since 2008. Her first book, *Mom Blogging for Dummies*, was authored in 2011. She has illustrated and/or published over 40 coloring and activity books for children and adults, including bestsellers *Coloring Flower Mandalas* (2015) and *The Drawing Book for Kids* (2017). She is the founder of Woo! Jr. Kids Activities, a media company with an audience of 50+ million and over 400,000 books sold. Her work has been featured on *The Today Show*, *The Huffington Post*, *The Wall Street Journal*, and Inc.com. She lives with her husband and family in Woodstock, IL.

Don't Stop Now...
Make Your Own Mandala Grids!

Making your own mandala grid is easy!
All you need is a ruler, a compass, a protractor, and a pencil.

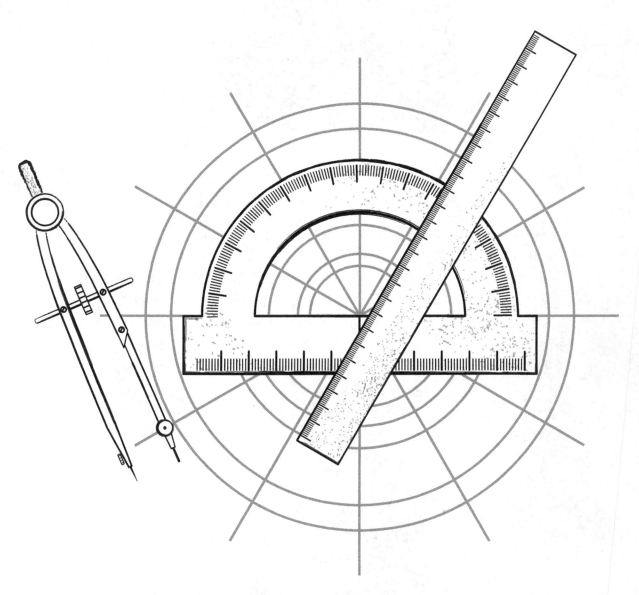

Draw a group of concentric circles (circles that share the same center point). Then use a centered protractor to mark angles at even intervals. Finally, draw each circle's radius with a ruler to mark the sections of your mandala. Use all of your ideas from this book to continue to draw mandalas to your heart's content!

CPSIA information can be obtained
at www.ICGtesting.com
Printed in the USA
JSHW040006060622
26712JS00004BA/33